POLYAMOROUS INTIMACY:

Polysecure Attachments practices, Trauma Healing, Thriving in Consensual Nonmonogamy Relationship and Emotional Security.

By

Tina C. Garner

Table of Contents

What is in this Book

Welcome to "Polysecure," a journey into the intricate dance of love, attachment, and consensual nonmonogamy (CNM). Picture this: a relationship landscape as diverse as a thriving ecosystem, where the roots of polyfidelity intertwine with the branches of secure attachment. In these pages, we unravel the tapestry of polyamorous connections, exploring the delicate threads that bind hearts across multiple bonds.

Ever wondered how attachment theory fits into the world of ethical nonmonogamy? Brace yourself for a rollercoaster ride through the highs of secure attachment, the twists of anxious longing, and the turns of avoidant independence. We're not just talking about love triangles here; we're diving deep into the polyamorous ocean, where the currents of communication, trust, and jealousy shape the very essence of our relationships.

But it's not all sunshine and rainbows. Trauma lurks in the shadows, affecting the foundations of our polyamorous castles. In "Polysecure," we confront the shadows, exploring how trauma impacts consensual nonmonogamy and offering a compass for healing.

Whether you're a seasoned polyamorist or a curious newcomer, these pages invite you into a world where love knows no bounds and attachment dances on the edge of possibility. Join us on this exploration of polysecure connections, where the heart's capacity for love defies traditional norms and embraces the rich tapestry of consensual nonmonogamy.

Scope and Objectives of the Book

Alright, let's dive into what this book is all about – consider this your backstage pass to the world of Polysecure relationships. You're probably wondering, "What's the deal here?" Well, buckle up, because we're on a journey to unravel the fascinating interplay between attachment, trauma, and consensual nonmonogamy.

Scope:

So, what's in our scope? Picture this book as a compass guiding you through the uncharted territories of relationships that aren't bound by traditional monogamy. We're not just skimming the surface; we're plunging into the deep waters of attachment theory and its connection to the world of nonmonogamous love. From the basics of attachment styles to the nitty-gritty of trauma-informed perspectives, we're leaving no stone unturned.

But hey, it's not just theory; we're diving into the real-world stuff. Case studies, examples, and anecdotes – we're unpacking the experiences of folks navigating Polysecure relationships. So, whether you're dipping your toes into the poly pool or you're already doing the backstroke, this book has something for everyone.

Objectives:

Now, let's talk objectives. We're not here to dictate how you should live your love life. Nope. Our goal is to equip you with the tools, insights, and aha moments to make your own informed decisions. We want you to understand the impact of attachment on your nonmonogamous journey, recognize the role of trauma, and, most importantly, foster healthier connections.

Communication is our secret weapon. We're arming you with strategies that go beyond the standard "we need to talk." It's about building a language of trust, openness, and understanding in the poly universe. Think of it as your polyamorous phrasebook – because sometimes, "I need space" just doesn't cut it.

But wait, there's more! We're not only exploring the challenges but also offering solutions. Jealousy, insecurity, conflicts – we're handing you a roadmap to navigate the bumps in the poly road. And yes, we're throwing in a dash of cultural and societal perspectives because, let's face it, love doesn't happen in a vacuum. We're considering the broader picture too.

So, grab your curiosity and a cup of your favorite beverage. Whether you're a seasoned poly pro or a newbie feeling like a fish out of water, this book is your companion, your confidante, and your guide to a world where love knows no bounds. Ready to embark on this adventure with us? Let's go!

Glossary of Terms

Hey there! So, you've dived into the world of Polysecure, and as you navigate the twists and turns of consensual nonmonogamy, you might encounter some terms that sound like they belong in a secret society. Fear not! We've got your back with a friendly guide to the language of Polysecure relationships.

***Polysecure (adj.)**
Definition: A state of emotional security within polyamorous or consensually nonmonogamous relationships. It's like the warm fuzzy feeling of knowing your favorite blanket is always there for you.

***Attachment Theory**
Definition: The psychological framework that explores how we form emotional bonds with others. It's like the instruction manual for understanding the intricate dance of human connection.

***Polyfidelity (n.)**
Definition: A form of consensual nonmonogamy where a group of individuals commit exclusively to

each other. Think of it as having a tight-knit, love-filled squad that's all about mutual exclusivity.

*Trauma-Informed

Definition: An approach that recognizes the impact of past experiences on an individual's well-being. It's like understanding that everyone comes with their own unique set of battle scars and that shapes who they are.

*Consensual Nonmonogamy (CNM)

Definition: A relationship style where all parties involved agree to engage romantically and/or sexually with others. It's like relationship freedom with a side of open communication and mutual respect.

*Anxious Attachment

Definition: A style where individuals crave closeness and worry about the stability of their relationships. It's like wanting to be wrapped in a cozy blanket of love but being afraid someone might accidentally yank it away.

***Avoidant Attachment**

Definition: A style where individuals value independence and may struggle with emotional intimacy. It's like having your emotional space, and you're not too keen on anyone barging in unannounced.

***Secure Attachment**

Definition: A style where individuals feel comfortable with both intimacy and independence. It's like having a relationship GPS that always guides you back to a comforting home base.

***Polysecure Parenting**

Definition: Navigating the joys and challenges of parenting within a consensually nonmonogamous family structure. It's like juggling parenting duties while maintaining a harmonious and loving household.

***Envisioning Healthy Futures**

Definition: Imagining the possibilities and growth within Polysecure relationships. It's like looking ahead to a world where love, communication, and understanding thrive in all their diverse forms.

So, there you have it! Your cheat sheet to the language of Polysecure. As you continue exploring the pages of this book, feel free to flip back here whenever you encounter a term that makes you go, "Wait, what does that mean again?" Happy reading, fellow adventurer!

Introduction

As we go into the fascinating world of Polysecure Relationships. It's not as complex as it might sound – in fact, think of it as your guide to creating strong, secure connections in the realm of consensual nonmonogamy.

So, what's the deal with Polysecure Relationships? Picture your typical relationship, but throw in some extra love, trust, and a dash of adventure. Polysecure relationships are all about breaking free from the traditional mold and embracing the idea that love and connection can extend beyond just one person.

Now, let's get down to the nitty-gritty. Polysecure relationships are built on a foundation of attachment. Think of attachment like the glue that holds relationships together – it's the emotional bond we share with our partners. In the world of nonmonogamy, this attachment becomes even more crucial. It's not just about you and your significant other; it's about navigating multiple connections, each with its unique flavor.

You know that feeling of security you get when your partner sends you a sweet text or holds your hand? Well, in a Polysecure Relationship, it's like having a whole network of support and affection. It's not just about one person meeting all your needs; it's about a community of connections, each contributing to your emotional well-being.

But, and it's a big but, understanding and navigating polysecure relationships requires some serious communication skills. Imagine juggling multiple conversations, desires, and boundaries – it's like orchestrating a symphony of emotions. Open and honest communication is the key to unlocking the full potential of a polysecure connection. Talk about your feelings, fears, and fantasies – lay it all out on the table.

Now, let's tackle the big question: how does attachment fit into all this? Well, it's like the secret sauce. Each person in a polysecure relationship forms unique attachment bonds with their various partners. It's not a competition; it's a collaboration of emotional connections. Understanding your attachment style and your partner's helps navigate the sometimes choppy waters of nonmonogamy.

Sure, challenges may arise – jealousy might knock on your door, or insecurities might try to creep in. That's where the magic of attachment comes in. Polysecure relationships are like a support system on steroids. It's not about sweeping issues under the rug but facing them head-on, together.

In the end, Polysecure Relationships are an evolving journey. It's not a destination but a continuous exploration of love, connection, and self-discovery. So, buckle up and enjoy the ride – the world of polysecure relationships is full of surprises, growth, and a whole lot of love.

Chapter 1: Attachment Theory Primer

Ever notice how some relationships just click, while others feel like they're missing a puzzle piece? Enter the Attachment Theory Primer – think of it as Relationship 101 but with a twist. Picture this: we're all wired to connect, thanks to these invisible strings called attachment. You've got Secure folks who are the human equivalent of steady rocks. Anxious folks might be a tad clingy, like a koala hugging a tree, while Avoidant ones? Well, they're the lone wolves, right? This primer breaks down these attachment styles like your favorite playlist – easy to understand, but with profound impact.

Imagine your relationship as a dance floor. Attachment styles lead this intricate dance, dictating the rhythm of connection. We explore the roots of attachment, its impact on your love groove, and why some relationships samba while others do the cha-cha of drama. No psych degree is needed, just a curiosity about why we vibe or collide in the dance of love. So, grab your dance shoes, and let's waltz through the enchanting world of Attachment Theory

– where the science of connection meets the poetry of relationships.

Basics of Attachment

Basics of Attachment: Navigating the Dance of Human Connection

Alright, let's go into the intriguing world of attachment—no rocket science here, just the nitty-gritty of how humans connect and bond. Imagine it as the invisible glue that sticks us together in relationships, friendships, and everything in between. It's like our social superpower, and we all wield it, knowingly or not.

The Need for Human Velcro

So, why do we attach? Well, imagine being a tiny human, fresh into this big, bustling world. You're not exactly equipped to fend off lions or build shelters. You need someone—a caregiver, usually—to keep you safe, fed, and cozy. That's where attachment kicks in. It's the baby's way of saying, "Hey, you, with the warm hugs and the milk, I choose you as my person."

Attachment Styles 101

Now, buckle up for a bit of psych-talk. There are different attachment styles, like a personality test for how we relate to others. First up, there's the Secure Attachment crew. These folks had caregivers who were consistent, responsive, and basically nailed the whole "trustworthy companion" gig.

Then, we have the Anxious-Preoccupied bunch. Picture a relational tightrope walk. They crave intimacy but are a tad worried it might slip away. On the flip side, there are the Avoidant types. They're the "I love you, but please don't get too close" squad, often due to inconsistent caregiving in their early years. And, of course, there's the Fearful-Avoidant, who might ping-pong between craving closeness and fearing it like a haunted house ride.

Impact on Grown-Up Relationships

Fast forward to adulthood. Your attachment style becomes your relational compass. Secure attachers generally glide through relationships with ease, trusting their partners and themselves. Anxious attachers might need a few more reassuring texts, while avoidant attachers might need space like a cat claiming its territory. But here's the plot twist: attachment styles can evolve. We're not stuck in the script we were handed as kids. With a dash of self-awareness and a sprinkle of personal growth, you can rewrite your relational story.

Attachment in the Wild: Friendships, Romances, and Beyond

Attachments aren't just for lovey-dovey stuff. Think about your best friend or colleague you can always count on. Yup, that's attachment doing its magic. It's the secret sauce in our support networks, helping us weather life's storms and celebrate its victories.
Now, let's talk about romance. Ever wonder why you feel that electric jolt when you meet someone special? Attachment is at play, my friend. It's that invisible force saying, "Hey, this person might just be your lobster" (cue the "Friends" reference).

The Art of Attachment Healing

What if your attachment history resembles a soap opera plot? Don't fret; there's hope. Attachment healing is like a spa day for your emotional well-being. It involves understanding your patterns, rewiring your brain a bit, and learning to dance through relationships with a newfound grace.

Remember, attachment isn't a one-size-fits-all deal. It's a bespoke suit tailored to your life experiences. So, as you navigate the intricate dance of human connection, embrace the quirks of your attachment style, and maybe, just maybe, learn to foxtrot with a little more finesse.

Attachment Styles

Attachment styles – those subtle, intricate blueprints etched into the fabric of our emotional connections. Think of them as the DNA of our relationships, shaping how we approach love, trust, and vulnerability.

Imagine your attachment style as the unique dance moves you've picked up in the ballroom of life. Are you a confident tango enthusiast, twirling through relationships with grace? Or perhaps more of a cautious two-stepper, carefully navigating the steps of emotional connection? Attachment styles, my friend, are like the choreography of our hearts.

First, let's talk about the Secure Attachment style. Picture this: you're the person who grew up with caregivers who were the steady background music to your life. They were there when you needed them, responsive to your cries or giggles, creating a foundation of trust. Secure attachers waltz through life with a sense of confidence. They believe in love, have an easy time giving and receiving affection, and generally feel pretty secure in their relationships.

Now, for the Anxious-Preoccupied Attachment style – the passionate salsa dancers of the attachment world. If this is you, you might have a tendency to crave closeness and worry about your partner's feelings for you. Your dance can sometimes be a bit intense, fueled by a fear of abandonment. Picture passionate spins and dips – that's the anxious-preoccupied dance, always craving reassurance and affection.

On the flip side, we have the Avoidant Attachment style – the solo breakdancers of the attachment spectrum. If you lean this way, you're likely to value independence and freedom. Attachment? You might prefer to keep it light, avoiding the deep emotional embraces. You've got some slick moves, but getting too close might make you want to break into a solo routine. Not because you don't care, but because you've learned to rely on yourself.

Now, let's throw in a mix: the Fearful-Avoidant Attachment style – the interpretative dancers. Ever seen those performers who mix elements of all dance styles? That's the fearful-avoidant, an intricate dance of conflicting desires. One moment they're reaching out for connection, the next they're pulling away. It's a dance of contradictions, a beautiful chaos of wanting and fearing closeness.

Think of these attachment styles as dance lessons for the heart. We all come into the ballroom with different experiences, different teachers, and different rhythms. The exciting part? You're not stuck with one dance style for life. With a bit of self-awareness and practice, you can refine your moves, switch up your dance, and even waltz into a more secure attachment style.

So, there you have it – the attachment styles, the unique dances that shape the way we live and connect. Whether you're twirling through life with a secure waltz, salsa-ing through passion, breakdancing through independence, or interpretative dancing through the complexities of fear and desire, remember: it's your dance, your rhythm, and the ballroom is yours to explore.

Impact of Attachment on Relationships

Ever noticed how relationships can be like a dance? Sometimes it's a graceful waltz, and other times, it's a chaotic tango. Well, here's a little secret – the dance floor is heavily influenced by something called attachment. It's like the music playing in the background, setting the rhythm for our romantic moves.

So, what's this attachment thing? It's not just about clinginess or independence; it's the emotional glue that binds us to others. Imagine it as a dance partner that you can't see but whose steps you can definitely feel.

In the beginning, attachment is like the first notes of a melody. It's the sweet, tentative hum of connection when you meet someone special. You start learning the steps, figuring out each other's moves. It's the thrill of a new dance, and you're twirling into the world of shared laughter and secrets.

As the dance progresses, you might find yourself swaying to the rhythm of secure attachment. It's like a harmonious duet where you both feel safe and supported. You trust your partner to lead, and they trust you to follow. This security allows the dance to flow effortlessly, creating a bond that can weather any storm.

But, ah, there's always a twist, isn't there? If early experiences left you with a shaky dance foundation – maybe you stumbled through steps marked by inconsistency or absence – you might find yourself doing a cha-cha of anxious attachment. It's that feeling of constantly seeking reassurance, wondering if your dance partner will disappear from the floor.

Then there's the tango of avoidant attachment. Picture someone taking a step back every time you try to get closer. It's not that they don't want to dance with you; they just need a bit more space. The dance becomes a delicate negotiation of closeness and distance.

Now, here's the plot twist – we don't always dance the same way with everyone. Attachment patterns can shift depending on the partner and the music of life playing in the background. It's like adapting your dance style to different beats.

Attachment also influences how we handle conflict. In a securely attached dance, disagreements are more like a brief misstep than a full-blown stumble. You recover gracefully, knowing the dance will continue. Anxiously attached dancers might fear the dance is ending, while avoidantly attached ones might retreat to a solo routine, needing time to regroup.

Here's the real kicker – awareness of your own attachment style can transform the dance floor dynamics. It's like suddenly understanding the rhythm of the music. You start leading or following with intention, creating a dance that's uniquely yours. It's about finding a balance between connection and independence, recognizing that the dance is a joint creation.

So, the next time you find yourself on the relationship dance floor, pay attention to the attachment notes in the background. Embrace the sway of secure attachment, navigate the dips of anxious or avoidant steps, and remember, it's your dance, your story. The music may change, but how you move to it is entirely up to you.

Importance of Attachment in Nonmonogamous Dynamics

Let's dive straight into the real nitty-gritty, the beating heart of nonmonogamy – attachment. Yeah, I know, it sounds a bit like psych lingo, but trust me, it's the secret sauce that makes or breaks the whole deal.

So, what's this attachment thing anyway? Picture it like the invisible string connecting you to your favorite people, creating a bond that's stronger than super glue. Now, in nonmonogamous relationships, it's not just about one string but a whole web of connections.

Attachments are the emotional glue holding together our relationships, whether they're traditional, open, or somewhere in the vast, uncharted land of nonmonogamy. And let me tell you, this stuff goes deep. It's not just about cozy Netflix nights and shared dog walks. Attachment is the backbone of the whole shebang.

Think about it. When you've got multiple partners in the mix, each with their quirks and charms, the attachment game gets seriously complex. You're not just managing your connection with one person; you're juggling a dynamic network of emotions, desires, and vulnerabilities. It's like playing emotional chess but without the rulebook.

Attachment styles come into play here – you know, those patterns we've picked up from childhood about how we connect with others. Are you the secure type, feeling pretty chill about your partner doing their own thing? Or maybe you're more of the anxious type, worrying if they'll forget to text back?

Nonmonogamous dynamics, my friend, put your attachment style front and center. They amplify the feelings. But hey, it's not all drama. Understanding your attachment style and your partner's is like having a roadmap for navigating the emotional rollercoaster of multiple connections.

Let's be real; it's not always sunshine and rainbows. Nonmonogamous setups can trigger some serious attachment insecurities. Jealousy might show up uninvited, and it's not the most pleasant guest at the party. But, and it's a big but, acknowledging these insecurities is the first step to dealing with them.

Communication – the superhero of every relationship – becomes the golden ticket in nonmonogamous dynamics. Talk about your fears, your needs, your hopes. Lay it all out on the table like a potluck dinner of emotions. It's vulnerability on steroids, and yeah, it's scary, but it's also the magic potion for creating stronger, more secure attachments.

Nonmonogamy is like a dance. It requires rhythm, communication, and a hell of a lot of trust. Attachment is the dance floor, and each step, misstep, and twirl contributes to the intricate choreography of your relationships.

And here's the kicker – nonmonogamous dynamics demand a level of self-awareness that's off the charts. You're not just exploring the depths of connection with others; you're diving deep into your own emotional ocean. It's a journey, an adventure, and a challenge all rolled into one messy, beautiful ball of human connection.

So, buckle up, my friend. We're about to explore the wild, wonderful world of attachment in nonmonogamous relationships, where the heart leads, and emotions take center stage. Get ready for a rollercoaster ride of self-discovery, intimacy, and a whole lot of love.

Chapter 2: Unpacking Trauma

Trauma, it's like this uninvited guest that crashes the party of your life and leaves a mess that you never signed up for. Imagine packing your suitcase for a journey, and trauma sneaks in, adding extra baggage you never wanted. Unpacking that trauma is like sorting through a chaotic suitcase. It's not just about tossing things out; it's about examining each item – the memories, the pain, the scars. Some things might be worn and tattered, but they hold stories. It's a messy process, like digging through a thrift store of emotions. Each layer peeled back reveals another layer of your story, and some parts are harder to confront than others. It's not about discarding everything; it's about deciding what you want to carry forward and what you're ready to let go. It's a journey, not a sprint, and sometimes you find unexpected treasures in the midst of the mess.

Trauma and Its Manifestations

Trauma and Its Sneaky Ways of Showing Up

Let's talk about trauma. It's not the easiest subject to dive into, but it's a real, tangible thing that affects more people than we might think. Trauma isn't just a buzzword; it's a silent guest at the dinner table of our lives, often showing up uninvited and lingering in the corners of our minds.

You know how they say "time heals all wounds"? Well, they might have left out a crucial detail: not all wounds heal the same way. Some scars, invisible to the eye, stick around, playing hide and seek with our emotions.

Imagine trauma as an uninvited guest crashing a party. It doesn't announce itself at the door; instead, it sneaks in, sipping on your emotional punch without you even realizing it. Then, when you least expect it, bam! It will now mess up everything.

One of trauma's favorite hiding spots is in our bodies. It's like a shape-shifter, taking on different forms – tension in the shoulders, that knot in your stomach, or the rapid heartbeat that seems to have a mind of its own. You might not even connect the dots between the fender bender you had last year and the way your palms still get sweaty when you hear screeching brakes.

Trauma isn't always about the big, dramatic events either. It can be a series of small, seemingly insignificant moments that add up over time. It's like a collection of puzzle pieces, each one representing a moment that left a mark. When you finally start putting the puzzle together, you realize it forms a picture you didn't expect.

Have you ever noticed how trauma has this eerie ability to play tricks on memory? It's like a master illusionist, distorting reality and leaving you questioning what really happened. You find yourself in a mental maze, trying to navigate through the fog of distorted recollections.

But here's the kicker: trauma isn't just about the past. It's a time traveler, showing up unannounced in your present moments. It whispers in your ear, triggering reactions that feel disproportionate to the situation at hand. That heated argument over dirty dishes? It might not be about the dishes at all; it could be trauma pulling the strings, dancing to a tune only it can hear.

And let's not forget about the sleepless nights. Trauma loves to be a night owl, lurking in the shadows when the world is quiet. It wakes you up with a start, replaying scenes you thought were long buried. Sleep becomes a battleground, and your dreams – well, they might as well be directed by Quentin Tarantino.

So, how do you deal with this uninvited, shape-shifting, time-traveling guest called trauma? The answer isn't one-size-fits-all, but it starts with acknowledging its presence. Shine a light on the corners where it likes to hide. Talk about it – not in hushed tones, but in your own authentic voice.

Because, my friend, understanding trauma is like unraveling a mystery. It's messy, it's complicated, but it's also a journey toward reclaiming pieces of yourself. So, let's talk about it, openly and honestly, because in that conversation lies the power to take back control from the uninvited guest who has overstayed its welcome.

Trauma-Informed Approaches in Relationships

Imagine relationships as delicate ecosystems, thriving on the delicate balance of emotions, trust, and vulnerability. Now, throw trauma into the mix - a wild card that can disrupt the harmony, leaving partners navigating uncharted territories. In this rollercoaster called life, adopting trauma-informed approaches in relationships becomes our compass, helping us find our way back to connection, understanding, and most importantly, healing.

So, what exactly does it mean to be trauma-informed in your relationship? Picture it like this: you're on a journey with your partner, and you both have baggage. Trauma-informed means acknowledging that baggage exists and being mindful of how it might show up in your relationship without blaming each other for the weight you carry.

First and foremost, it's about creating a safe space – a haven where both of you can be raw, real, and a little messy. Think of it as a cozy living room with metaphorical blankets and cushions, providing comfort and assurance. When your partner feels safe, they're more likely to open up about their past, share their fears, and let you into the labyrinth of their emotions.

Communication takes center stage in trauma-informed relationships. It's not just about talking; it's about really listening. Imagine you're not just hearing words but tuning into the emotions behind them. Sometimes, it's the unspoken that holds the weight. So, toss out the notion of mind-reading and replace it with a genuine curiosity about your partner's thoughts and feelings.

Now, let's talk triggers. We all have them, those emotional landmines waiting to be unintentionally stepped on. Trauma-informed love means understanding each other's triggers and creating a roadmap to navigate around them. Picture it as a treasure map, with 'X' marking the spots where you should tread lightly. When your partner feels you're attuned to their triggers, it builds a bridge of trust, and bridges are what keep relationships strong.

Patience, dear reader, is the secret sauce in trauma-informed relationships. Healing is a marathon, not a sprint. Picture it like growing a garden – you plant the seeds, water them, and patiently wait for the first bloom. Relationships are no different. Give each other the time and space to heal, and watch your love garden flourish.

Here's a radical thought: what if we redefine strength in relationships? In a trauma-informed paradigm, strength is not about being invincible; it's about vulnerability. It's about admitting when you're not okay and trusting your partner enough to say, "Hey, I need you right now." Vulnerability is the glue that binds couples in a trauma-informed dance, where the steps are syncopated with love, compassion, and mutual support.

So, as you journey through the labyrinth of love, armed with the compass of trauma-informed approaches, remember this: the destination isn't a utopian relationship free of flaws. It's a connection where both partners, flawed and beautifully human, find solace in each other's arms. There's no script, no one-size-fits-all guide; it's an ever-evolving dance, with both of you leading and following, stumbling and twirling through the rhythm of shared vulnerability.

In the end, it's not about avoiding the storms but learning to dance in the rain together.

Healing Trauma within Polyamorous Structures

Healing Trauma within Polyamorous Structures: A Compassionate Journey

Let's explore into a realm that's as real as your morning coffee – healing trauma in the world of polyamory. Yeah, we're getting cozy with the tough stuff, but don't worry; we're doing it with a cup of empathy and a sprinkle of understanding.

Picture this: You're cruising through the seas of polyamorous connections, embracing love in multiple forms. It's all sunshine and rainbows until, bam, the storm hits – trauma. It's the rogue wave you didn't see coming, and suddenly, those waters aren't as crystal clear anymore.

So, how do you navigate this tumultuous sea of emotions and past hurts within the tapestry of polyamorous relationships? Well, grab your life jacket, because we're setting sail.

**Acknowledging the Emotional Weather Report
First things first, we need to be weather watchers of our emotions. What's brewing beneath the surface? Recognizing the storm clouds of past trauma is crucial. Maybe it's an old heartbreak or the echoes of a relationship that left you battered. Acknowledging these emotional weather patterns is your compass – it tells you where you've been and where you need to steer.

**Communication: The Wind in Your Sails
Now, let's talk about the wind in your sails – communication. In polyamory, it's the force that propels you forward. Opening up about your struggles, fears, and triggers is like adjusting the sails to weather the storm. It's not about blame or pointing fingers; it's about saying, "Hey, I've got some baggage on board. Can we navigate this together?"

Navigating Choppy Waters: Patience and Understanding

Healing trauma in polyamorous structures is a slow dance, not a sprint. It's about holding hands while wading through the choppy waters. Patience becomes your anchor, and understanding is your lifeboat. Sometimes, it's about sitting in the discomfort and saying, "I see you, I hear you, and we'll get through this together."

Building Safe Harbors: Boundaries and Consent

In the midst of healing, boundaries become your lighthouse. Establishing clear limits is like drawing a map – it shows where the safe harbors are. Consent is the anchor dropped in those safe harbors, ensuring that everyone is on board with the journey. It's not about restriction; it's about creating spaces where healing can thrive.

The Crew Matters Support Systems in Polyamory

You're not sailing these seas alone. Your polyamorous crew matters. They're the ones who throw you a lifebuoy when the waves get too high. Whether it's a reassuring word, a warm hug, or just a knowing glance, your support system is the heart of your journey. It's the 'we' in 'we'll get through this.'

**Embracing the Rainbow After the Storm

As you navigate the waters of healing trauma in polyamorous structures, don't forget to look for the rainbow after the storm. It's not about erasing the scars but transforming them into a kaleidoscope of resilience. Each wave of healing brings a new shade to your relationship canvas, creating a masterpiece of strength, vulnerability, and love.

So, there you have it – a guide to healing trauma in the realm of polyamory. It's a journey that requires courage, compassion, and a willingness to navigate the unpredictable seas of the heart. But remember, in the end, it's not about reaching a conclusion; it's about embracing the ongoing adventure of growth, connection, and healing.

Chapter 3: Polyfidelity

Welcome to the Polyfidelity playground! This chapter is like the VIP section of the consensual nonmonogamy party. So, what's the deal with Polyfidelity? Think of it as a committed group hug—imagine a small, tight-knit circle of folks who've decided, "Hey, we're in this together!" It's not your run-of-the-mill polyamory; it's like building a love fort with a select few. We'll dive into the perks and challenges of this exclusive love club, exploring why some folks choose it over the traditional poly route. Ever wondered how to balance intimacy in a group setting? We've got you covered! From defining boundaries to navigating emotional roller coasters, this chapter is your Polyfidelity handbook. Get ready for some serious relationship insights and a backstage pass to the CNM experience you never knew existed. Buckle up, because we're about to unravel the mysteries of love, trust, and commitment in a way you've never seen before!

Definition and Exploration of Polyfidelity

Imagine your love life is a dynamic, ever-evolving dance, and suddenly you find yourself engaged in a waltz with not one, not two, but a handful of partners. Welcome to the realm of polyfidelity, a fascinating concept that turns the conventional notion of monogamy on its head.

***Polyfidelity Unveiled: Beyond Monogamous Boundaries**

So, what on earth is polyfidelity? Let's break it down without getting tangled in a web of jargon. Polyfidelity is like having a tight-knit love posse—a committed group where everyone involved is romantically and intimately connected. Picture it as a love squad, a chosen family, or a relationship Avengers team where trust, communication, and mutual understanding are the superpowers.

***It's Not a Love Free-for-All, It's a Love Exclusive Club**

Polyfidelity isn't a wild, anything-goes, love free-for-all. It's more like an exclusive club where the members are dedicated to each other. In this club, there's a pact, an unspoken agreement that says, "Hey, we're in this together, and our love is the real deal." It's not about collecting romantic conquests like Pokémon; it's about cultivating a deep, meaningful connection with a select few.

***Polyamory Plus Commitment: The Power Combo**

Now, your thought might be, "Isn't it just polyamory?" Well, not quite. Polyfidelity is like the superhero version of polyamory—it's polyamory with a cape. In polyamory, you might have multiple relationships, but they can operate independently. In polyfidelity, there's a commitment to the group as a whole. It's not just about one-on-one connections; it's about the collective energy of the entire polyfidelitous crew.

***Communication, Trust, and the Polyfidelity Playbook**

In the land of polyfidelity, communication is the glue that holds everything together. Picture a team of superheroes coordinating their moves in a battle; that's how essential communication is in a polyfidelitous relationship. There's a playbook, an unwritten guide that emphasizes openness, honesty, and active listening. Because, let's face it, you can't save the day if you're not on the same page.

***Navigating Jealousy: The Kryptonite of Polyfidelity**

Now, let's talk about the Kryptonite of any superhero squad—jealousy. In polyfidelity, it's a real and present danger. But fear not, intrepid reader, for the polyfidelity crew has a secret weapon: compersion. Compersion is the joy you feel when your partner find happiness with others. It's like cheering on your teammates even when they score a point with someone else. It's not just about your victories; it's about celebrating the victories of the entire squad.

***Polyfidelity: Not for the Faint of Heart, but Oh So Rewarding**

In this love adventure called polyfidelity, it's not always smooth sailing. It requires a level of commitment and self-awareness that might make some people hesitate. But for those who dive in, the rewards are unparalleled. It's a journey of self-discovery, a saga of building something unique and extraordinary with a group of people who become more than just partners—they become family.

So, there you have it—a glimpse into the vibrant, complex world of polyfidelity. It's not a fairy tale, and it's not a utopia, but for those who dare to explore its depths, it's a love story that transcends the ordinary. In the grand tapestry of human connection, polyfidelity adds a splash of color, a kaleidoscope of emotions, and a reminder that love, in all its forms, is the true superhero of our stories.

Benefits of Polyfidelity in Consensual Nonmonogamy (CNM)

Alright, imagine this: You're navigating the intricate dance of love, and traditional monogamy just doesn't seem to fit the rhythm of your heart. Enter polyfidelity, the unsung hero in the world of Consensual Nonmonogamy (CNM). Buckle up, because we're about to explore the wild ride of benefits that polyfidelity brings to the relationship table.

1. Team Love: The More, the Merrier

Ever felt like your heart was just too darn big to be contained by one person? Polyfidelity steps in like the cool friend who says, "Why limit yourself?" In this setup, a group of committed individuals forms a close-knit team, sharing love, support, and joy. It's like having your own personal squad cheering you on in the game of life.

2. Security Blanket for the Heart

Picture this: you're snuggled up in bed, surrounded by the warmth of multiple partners who've got your back. Polyfidelity provides a unique sense of security that goes beyond the traditional norms. It's like having a heart-shaped security blanket made of emotional support, loyalty, and a bunch of "I've got you, always" promises.

3. Communication Olympics: Gold Medal Edition

Ever tried juggling multiple conversations, feelings, and schedules? It's like a communication Olympics, and polyfidelity turns you into the gold medalist. With open and honest dialogue at its core, this arrangement forces you to become a master communicator. Forget the silent treatment; here, everyone's a chatterbox of emotions, needs, and desires.

4. Variety is the Spice of Love Life

Monotony in relationships is so last season. Polyfidelity adds a dash of spice to your love life, offering a variety that's like having a buffet of romantic experiences. Different partners bring different flavors, and suddenly, your love life becomes a tantalizing journey through diverse connections and intimate moments.

5. Shared Responsibilities, Shared Bliss

Remember the saying, "Many hands make light work"? In polyfidelity, it's more like "Many hearts make light love." Shared responsibilities don't just refer to chores; they extend to emotional support, problem-solving, and the celebration of each other's victories. It's a collective effort to create a harmonious love symphony.

6. Jealousy, Meet Your Match

Jealousy, the notorious troublemaker in many relationships, takes a backseat in polyfidelity. When everyone is on the same page, jealousy sulks away. It's not a competition; it's a collaboration. Partners support each other's connections, and jealousy finds itself replaced by compersion—the joy in witnessing your loved ones experiencing happiness.

7. Built-In Support System

Feeling overwhelmed? In polyfidelity, you're not alone. Your partners aren't just romantic interests; they're your built-in support system. From bad days at work to personal triumphs, you've got a cheering squad ready to lift you up. It's like having a family you've chosen, bound together by love and shared experiences.

8. Freedom to Evolve

Life is a journey, and so is love. Polyfidelity acknowledges that people grow and change. It's not about fitting into a predetermined mold but embracing the freedom to evolve. Each partner becomes a chapter in your love story, contributing to your personal growth and the vibrant tapestry of your romantic life.

Polyfidelity, in the realm of CNM, is like a bouquet of diverse flowers—each one unique, contributing to the beauty of the whole. It's a journey of self-discovery, shared experiences, and the boundless capacity of the human heart to love, connect, and thrive in a multitude of ways.

Challenges and Solutions of Polyfidelity in Consensual Nonmonogamy (CNM)

Navigating the waters of Polyfidelity in Consensual Nonmonogamy (CNM) can feel like embarking on a thrilling adventure. However, every adventurer knows that even the most exciting journeys come with their fair share of challenges. So, grab your compass, because we're about to explore the wild landscape of Polyfidelity and discover some ingenious ways to overcome the hurdles.

1. Juggling Multiple Connections:

Picture this: you've got your partner, your metamours, and maybe a few more in the mix. Suddenly, it's like orchestrating a polyamorous circus. The challenge? Balancing time and attention. The solution? It's all about communication and scheduling acrobatics. Create shared calendars, plan regular check-ins, and embrace the art of prioritizing without making anyone feel like they're in the nosebleed section of your life.

2. Jealousy in the Room:

Ah, the green-eyed monster – it loves to crash the poly party. Jealousy can sneak up on you when you least expect it, and it's a formidable opponent. To conquer this challenge, acknowledge it when it appears. Have open conversations about insecurities and fears. Sometimes, a simple acknowledgment and a reassuring hug can chase jealousy away faster than you can say "compersion."

3. Communication Breakdowns:

Communication is the glue holding any relationship together, and in Polyfidelity, it's like super glue. The challenge? Misunderstandings and crossed wires. The solution? Be a communication ninja. Practice active listening, ask clarifying questions, and don't be afraid to use "I" statements to express your feelings without pointing fingers. When everyone's on the same page, the story of your poly journey unfolds smoothly.

4. Nurturing Intimacy with Multiple Partners:

The challenge here is like trying to grow a garden with diverse plants – each one needs a specific kind of care. To overcome this, cultivate intentional intimacy. Schedule one-on-one time with each partner, create unique rituals or inside jokes, and foster a sense of exclusivity within the poly web. It's like having a bouquet of flowers, each one distinct but contributing to the beauty of the whole.

5. External Judgment and Social Stigma:

Unfortunately, we live in a world where not everyone is waving the polyamory flag. The challenge? Navigating societal judgment and misconceptions. The remedy? Arm yourself with a dash of indifference and a sprinkle of education. Share your story when you feel comfortable, challenge stereotypes, and surround yourself with a supportive community. Sometimes, the best defense is living your truth with confidence.

6. Different Relationship Styles Among Partners:

In Polyfidelity, not everyone follows the same relationship manual. The challenge arises when partners have different expectations. The solution? Embrace flexibility, have honest discussions about relationship structures, and find common ground.

Flexibility isn't a sign of weakness; it's the key to a harmonious poly dance.

7. Managing Emotional Baggage:

We all carry a bit of emotional luggage, right? In Polyfidelity, this baggage can occasionally spill over into your interconnected relationships. The key? Emotional intelligence and a touch of therapy magic. Encourage open discussions about past experiences, support each other in personal growth, and be ready to lend a hand (or a tissue) when someone needs to unpack their emotional suitcase.

8. Dealing with the Unexpected Curveballs:

Life loves throwing curveballs, and Polyfidelity is no exception. Unexpected situations can rattle the poly ship. The secret? Adaptability and a sturdy life jacket. Be ready to pivot, adjust sails, and navigate storms together. Resilience is the unsung hero of poly relationships.

Remember, the challenges of Polyfidelity are like the plot twists in a captivating novel – they keep the story interesting. Embrace them, learn from them, and most importantly, face them together with your poly crew. After all, it's the shared experiences, the victories, and even the missteps that make the poly adventure worth embarking on. So, tie your shoelaces, because the journey is ongoing, and the next chapter is always waiting to be written.

Chapter 4: The Landscape of Consensual Nonmonogamy

Navigating the landscape of consensual nonmonogamy is like setting sail on a relationship adventure with a compass that doesn't point due north. We're exploring the vast ocean of love, but this time, it's not just one ship—it's a flotilla. Polyamory, open relationships, and other nontraditional setups are the new normal. Imagine a dating world where honesty isn't just the best policy; it's the only one. It's not about sneaking around; it's about embracing a patchwork of connections. Picture a relational smorgasbord, where individuals create bespoke arrangements that challenge the cookie-cutter norms. Sure, there are challenges—waves of jealousy, storms of misunderstanding—but there's also this beautiful chaos of multiple connections, each with its own rhythm. In this dynamic seascape, consensual nonmonogamy isn't a rebellion; it's a celebration of love's boundless possibilities. The landscape might be uncharted, but oh, the stories we'll tell about the journey.

Types of Nonmonogamous Relationships

Alright, buckle up, because we're about to dive headfirst into the wild and wonderful world of nonmonogamous relationships. No, it's not just a buzzword – it's a whole spectrum of ways people choose to connect and love, and trust me, it's way more colorful than your average relationship flowchart.

1.The Rebel: Open Relationships
 So, picture this: your typical monogamous setup, but with a twist. Open relationships are like the mavericks of the dating scene. They dance to the beat of their own drum, allowing room for romantic connections outside the primary partnership. It's not about rebellion; it's about embracing a wider view of love.

2. The Dreamweaver: Polyamory
 Now, if open relationships are the rebels, polyamory is the Dreamweaver. This is where things get beautifully complex. Forget the one-size-fits-all love story; polyamorous folks are crafting intricate

narratives with multiple characters, each adding their own unique flavor to the plot. It's like a love buffet, and trust me, everyone's invited.

3. The Trailblazer: Relationship Anarchy

Ever felt suffocated by relationship labels? Relationship anarchists are nodding in agreement. These trailblazers toss aside traditional hierarchies and rules, opting for a more fluid, label-free existence. It's not chaos; it's an art form – painting love outside the lines.

4. The Maverick: Swinging

If you're into spontaneity and, let's say, a dash of adventure, swinging might be your jam. Swingers are like the thrill-seekers of nonmonogamy, exploring intimacy with others in a consensual, boundary-respecting dance. It's not about keys in a bowl; it's about embracing a different kind of social swing.

5. The Free Spirit: Solo Polyamory

For those who value independence as much as connection, solo polyamory is where it's at. These free spirits navigate the relationship landscape without the anchor of a primary partner, relishing in the freedom to explore connections on their terms. It's not about flying solo; it's about a symphony of connections that harmonize without a central conductor.

6. The Time Traveler: Parallel Polyamory
Ever wished you could clone yourself to experience more love? Well, parallel polyamorists are the closest thing to time travelers. They maintain multiple, separate relationships concurrently, each evolving independently. It's not about time management; it's about embracing the full spectrum of connections without compromise.

7. The Shape Shifter: Hybrid Models
Now, if you're feeling a bit overwhelmed by all these options, fear not. Many folks are out here crafting their unique, hybrid models of nonmonogamy. It's like creating your own relationship recipe, combining elements from various approaches to suit your taste. After all, love isn't one-size-fits-all – it's a DIY project.

So, there you have it – the types of nonmonogamous relationships, each a vibrant stroke in the masterpiece of love. Remember, no matter which path you choose, the key is communication, consent, and a whole lot of heart. Cheers to the adventurous journey ahead!

Historical Perspectives on Nonmonogamy

Now we're about to take a wild ride through the annals of history, where relationships weren't just black and white, but rather, a vibrant spectrum of love and connection.

Back in the Day: Love and Labyrinths
Picture this: ancient civilizations, where polyamory wasn't a buzzword but a way of life. Mesopotamians were probably sipping on some Babylonian brew, passing around dates and affection like it was the norm. If those ancient walls could talk, they'd spill the tea on love triangles, quadrangles, and more shapes than Euclid could dream up.

Medieval Mix-ups and Royal Remixes
Fast forward to the Middle Ages, where courtly love wasn't as straightforward as knights in shining armor and damsels in distress. Behind the castle

walls, royals were juggling relationships like jesters with flaming torches. Monogamy? That was just a suggestion for those with a penchant for simplicity.

Victorian Virtues and Secret Gardens
Oh, the Victorian era – where corsets were tight, and rules were tighter. But behind closed doors, secret gardens of desire flourished. Whispered scandals of mistresses, affairs, and unconventional entanglements echoed through the opulent halls. It turns out, that even when societal expectations frowned, the heart danced to its own rebellious tune.

The Jazz Age of Free Love
Fast forward to the Roaring Twenties – the jazz age, where flappers were breaking free from social norms, and love was anything but monotonous. Speakeasies weren't just serving up illegal hooch; they were also incubators for experimental relationships. The Great Gatsby may have been chasing green lights, but others were chasing a rainbow of love.

Hippies, Love-Ins, and Groovy Polyamory
The '60s and '70s brought us tie-dye, peace signs, and a revolution in love. Hippies weren't just

protesting; they were exploring the frontiers of nonmonogamy. Communes weren't just about sharing chores; they were about sharing affection and discovering love without boundaries.

Today's Remix: Swipe Right for Nonmonogamy
 Fast forward to the present, where our smartphones are our wingmen in the dance of love. Dating apps have become the modern-day agora, where individuals can navigate relationships with the swipe of a finger. Nonmonogamy isn't just a relic of the past; it's a dynamic, evolving force shaping our relationships in the 21st century.

So, here we are, standing on the shoulders of love pioneers, charting our course through the ever-shifting landscape of relationships. The historical perspectives on nonmonogamy are not dusty tales but vibrant stories, urging us to rethink, reimagine, and maybe rewrite the rules of love. After all, history has always been a playground for the rebels of the heart. Where to next? Well, that's a chapter still being written.

Challenges and Benefits of Consensual Nonmonogamy

Section 1: Buckle Up, It's Complicated

Ah, consensual nonmonogamy - it's like diving headfirst into a rollercoaster. First, let's talk about the loops and turns. You know, the Challenges. They're the dips that make your stomach churn and your heart race.

The Communication Tango: Picture this – multiple partners, different schedules, and everyone expecting clear communication. It's like orchestrating a symphony, but with emotions. We'll navigate the art of talking, listening, and decoding the messages between the lines.

Jealousy Junction: Ah, the green-eyed monster. It's not just a saying; it's a real thing. We'll explore jealousy's unexpected appearances and how to deal with it. Spoiler: it involves more than just counting to ten.

Navigating Society's Side-eye: Society can be a real buzzkill sometimes. We'll tackle the social stigma, raised eyebrows, and the "but isn't that just cheating?" questions. Get ready to perfect your witty comebacks.

Section 2: The Scenic Views

Now, let's switch gears and zoom in on the Benefits. Imagine the rollercoaster climbing to the top, giving you a breathtaking view. That's what these perks are - the moments that make it all worthwhile.

Relationship Renaissance: Multiple partners mean a variety of perspectives and experiences. It's similar to not having a set menu but rather a buffet. We'll explore how this diversity can spark personal growth and transform your approach to relationships.

Freedom in Flexibility: Forget the one-size-fits-all model. We'll dive into the flexibility of consensual nonmonogamy – how it allows relationships to evolve organically, adapting to the changing needs and desires of everyone involved.

Support Squad: Multiple partners mean multiple sources of support. We'll uncover how a consensually nonmonogamous setup can create a robust support network, providing comfort and camaraderie in ways that a traditional relationship might struggle to match.

Love, Love, Everywhere: Love isn't a finite resource. We'll delve into the abundance mindset, exploring how embracing love in its various forms can enrich your life and the lives of your partners.

So, fasten your seatbelt, dear reader. Consensual nonmonogamy isn't for the faint of heart, but the views from the top are nothing short of spectacular. Whether you're facing the Challenges or basking in the Benefits, this is one ride that promises to be unforgettable.

Chapter 5: Polysecure Foundations

Polysecure Foundations is like building a relationship house – a sturdy structure for your polyamorous journey. Imagine it as a manual with blueprints for crafting robust emotional connections. Learn how to lay the groundwork for secure attachments within the intricate landscape of multiple partners. We'll delve into the art of communication, offering tools for expressing needs and navigating tricky emotions. Picture it as a treasure map to navigate the treasure islands of jealousy and insecurity. Through relatable stories, discover how others have created their own Polysecure Foundations, and draw inspiration for your unique poly adventure. It's not just about love; it's about understanding how attachment styles shape your nonmonogamous dynamics. As we explore, consider this your personal guide, helping you construct a loving, supportive space where multiple hearts can thrive. This the construction zone of Polysecure Foundations – let's build something beautiful together!

Building Secure Attachments in Poly Relationships

So, you've decided to dive into the wild and wonderful world of polyamory. Buckle up, friend, because, in this chapter, we're laying down the bricks for something pretty darn important: building secure attachments in your poly relationships.

1. Setting the Scene: What's the Deal with Secure Attachments?
 Alright, let's start with the basics. Imagine a secure attachment as the cozy blanket fort of your childhood dreams. It's that safe space where you can be yourself, share your secrets, and know that someone's got your back. In poly relationships, this secure base is like the North Star guiding you through the galaxy of multiple connections.

2. Tools for Your Poly Toolkit
 Now, let's stock up your toolkit for relationship adventures. Communication is the MVP here. We're not talking about decoding ancient scrolls; just speak your truth. Be as clear as that crystal ball you wish

you had when navigating relationship dynamics. No mind-reading allowed—express those feelings and desires!

3. Jealousy: The Friendly Neighbor
 Ah, jealousy, the unwelcome guest at the polyamorous party. We're not pretending it doesn't exist; we're acknowledging its presence and giving it a seat at the table. Explore those feelings, understand where they're coming from, and work through them like a team of superheroes. You're not in this alone.

4. Trust: The Glue That Holds It All Together
 Picture trust as the super glue of your relationships. It's what makes everything stick, even when life throws curveballs. Trust your partners, trust yourself, and heck, trust the process. Building a trust-filled foundation is like crafting a love potion that stands the test of time.

5. Self-Care: Fueling Your Relationship Engine
 Just like a car needs gas to run smoothly, your relationships need a dose of self-care. Don't neglect yourself in the hustle and bustle of poly life. Take that bubble bath, binge-watch your guilty pleasure

show, and remember that self-love is the secret sauce to flourishing connections.

6. Vulnerability: The True Power Move

Opening up can be a bit like performing without a safety net, but that vulnerability is where the magic happens. It's the dance floor where intimate connections are formed. So, throw on your dancing shoes and let the authenticity shine. Be real, be you, and let your partners do the same.

7. The Polysecure Playlist: A Symphony of Connection

Every relationship needs a soundtrack. Create a playlist that celebrates your unique connections. From the high notes of joy to the low beats of challenges, let the music remind you that this poly journey is your personal symphony—a masterpiece in the making.

8. Embracing Imperfection: Your Relationship Canvas

Spoiler alert: perfection is overrated. Embrace the messiness, the quirks, and the beautifully imperfect strokes on your relationship canvas. Remember, you're not creating a flawless masterpiece; you're co-authoring a story with your partners—one that's real, raw, and utterly yours.

9. Navigating Stormy Weather: Conflict Resolution 101

Let's face it, storms happen. Disagreements are part of the human experience, especially in the poly realm. But fear not! Equip yourself with the tools of active listening, empathy, and compromise. Weathering the storm together is what strengthens the foundation of your relationships.

10. Gratitude: The Secret Sauce for Lasting Bonds

In the hustle of everyday life, it's easy to forget the magic in your connections. Take a moment to express gratitude for the unique qualities each partner brings to your world. Gratitude, my friend, is the sprinkle of stardust that keeps the love alive and thriving.

And there you have it—your guide to building secure attachments in your poly relationships. Remember, it's not about finding the perfect formula but discovering the unique alchemy that makes your connections special. So, go forth, create, love, and let the adventure unfold.

Communication Strategies for Polysecure Connections

Navigating the Polysecure Seas – Communication Unplugged

Alright, let's go into the nitty-gritty of communication in polysecure relationships. It's not rocket science, but it's an art, a dance, a delicate balancing act. Picture it like a high-wire act without a safety net—exciting, a bit nerve-wracking, but ultimately, it's about finding your groove and keeping the connection alive.

1. Speak Up, Listen Hard

First things first, open your mouth! The first step in communication is to convey your ideas and emotions. Don't be shy; your partner can't read your mind. If something's bugging you or making you do the happy dance, spill it. And here's the secret sauce: active listening. That means really tuning in, not just nodding while you plan your response. Let your partner know they're heard and understood.

2. The Art of Transparency

In the polysecure world, honesty isn't just the best policy; it's the only policy. Lay it all out on the table, fears, desires, quirky habits, and all. Transparency builds trust, and in polyamory, trust is the golden ticket. Think of it as a trust-fall exercise but with your emotions. It might be scary, but hey, there's a soft landing.

3. Embracing the Awkward Silence

Awkward silences—they happen. Instead of filling every quiet moment with nervous chatter, let them breathe. Sometimes the best conversations follow a pregnant pause. Use those moments to reflect, connect, and savor the richness of shared silence.

4. Emoji Talk – Beyond Words

Not all communication happens through words. Embrace the wonderful world of emojis, gifs, and memes. A well-timed heart emoji can say more than a thousand words. It's the modern-day love letter, condensed into a tiny digital expression. Plus, it adds a touch of playfulness to serious conversations.

5. The Check-In Ritual

Make check-ins a regular thing. Think of it as a relationship pit stop. How are you feeling? What's on your mind? Check the emotional fuel gauge. It doesn't have to be a grand production; a simple "How was your day?" can work wonders.

6. Weathering the Storms Together

Polysecure connections aren't always sunshine and rainbows. Storms happen—misunderstandings, jealousy, insecurities. When the tempest hits, weather it together. Use "I" statements to express feelings without pointing fingers, and remember, it's you and your partner against the problem, not against each other.

7. Flexibility – The Relationship Yoga Pose

Flexibility isn't just for yoga mats; it's a key player in polysecure relationships. Life is unpredictable, and relationships need to be bendy. Be open to adapting, renegotiating, and recalibrating. It's like a dance floor where the steps can change, but the music keeps playing.

8. Laughter – The Glue of Connection
 Finally, sprinkle in a healthy dose of laughter. Relationships can get heavy; humor is the helium that lifts you up. Whether it's a shared inside joke or a funny cat video, laughter eases tension and cements your connection.

So, there you have it—communication in the polysecure universe, where words, emojis, and laughter become the threads weaving your intricate relationship tapestry. Now, go out there and chat your way to polysecure bliss!

Chapter 6: Communication Strategies for Polysecure Relationships

Navigating the intricacies of Polysecure Relationships is like sailing uncharted waters – communication becomes your compass. Picture it as a shared map between partners, ensuring everyone's on the same page. Open and honest dialogue is your wind, propelling you forward. Start by discussing individual attachment needs. Imagine it as comparing travel itineraries; you want everyone's expectations clear. Negotiating boundaries? Think of it like drawing lines in the sand together, a collaborative effort where everyone's comfort matters. When the seas get stormy – and they might – it's crucial to weather the storm with effective communication. Picture it as finding refuge in each other's words, a shelter from the emotional tempest. Trust is your anchor; it keeps the ship steady. Like any journey, there'll be detours and scenic routes, but communication is your reliable guide, helping you explore the vast landscape of Polysecure Relationships with curiosity and understanding.

Open and Honest Communication

Open and Honest Communication: The Heartbeat of Connection

Hey there, fellow explorers of the tangled web of relationships! Let's dive into a fundamental aspect that can make or break any connection – open and honest communication. Picture this: your relationship is a ship navigating through the seas of life. What's the compass guiding you through stormy weather and calm seas alike? Yep, you guessed it – it's the fine art of talking straight from the heart.

The ABCs of Openness

Let's strip away the fancy jargon and get back to basics. Open communication is like oxygen for relationships. It's not just about talking; it's about expressing your thoughts, fears, and dreams without fear of judgment. It's creating a space where your partner feels safe to share the quirky, messy, and downright confusing parts of themselves.

When you're open, it's like leaving the door to your emotional living room wide open, inviting your partner to kick back on the couch and spill their thoughts. No judgment. No raised eyebrows. Just a safe space where vulnerability becomes the secret sauce that binds you together.

The Unfiltered Truth

Honesty, my friends, is the daring superhero of communication. It's not always easy to be brutally honest, especially when you're afraid of hurting feelings or facing the consequences of truth bombs. But let me tell you, honesty isn't about being brutal; it's about being real.

Imagine your relationship as a garden. Secrets and half-truths are like weeds – they might seem small, harmless even, but let them grow, and they'll choke the life out of your connection. Honesty, on the other hand, is the fertilizer that helps your love garden bloom. Sure, it might be a bit smelly at first, but the results are worth it.

The Nitty-Gritty of Real Talk

Now, let's talk about the nitty-gritty – the actual art of opening your mouth and letting those thoughts escape. It's not always about finding the perfect time or crafting a poetic soliloquy. Sometimes, it's about grabbing a cup of coffee, sitting down, and saying, "Hey, can we talk?"

Real talk: It's not just about expressing your feelings but also being a master of the equally crucial skill of listening. Have you ever been waiting for your turn to speak in a conversation?
 Yeah, that's not it. Real communication is a two-way street where both voices matter, and listening isn't just waiting for your turn to talk but truly absorbing what your partner is saying.

Navigating the Rapids of Disagreements
 Let's face it, not every conversation is a stroll in the park. Disagreements happen, and that's okay. It's not the disagreements that matter but how you navigate them. Imagine you're on a river, and instead of dodging the rocks, you paddle together through the rapids. Conflict becomes a journey you embark on hand in hand, not a battle to be won.

Sure, it might be uncomfortable at times, and emotions might surge like the rapids, but remember, it's a shared adventure. You don't have to agree on everything, but you do need to respect each other's viewpoint, like two hikers taking different trails but meeting at the summit.

The Power of "I" Statements
Let's talk about "I" – not the ego-stroking kind, but the powerful "I" statements that transform blame into understanding. Saying "I feel" instead of "You always" is the difference between a conversation and a confrontation. It's a subtle shift that can turn a potential argument into a constructive dialogue.

So, there you have it, fellow relationship enthusiasts – the crux of open and honest communication. It's not rocket science, but it's an art that requires practice, patience, and a willingness to bare your soul a little. Remember, communication is the heartbeat of connection, so keep those lines open, be real, and let the magic unfold. Happy communicating!

Negotiating Boundaries in Nonmonogamous Partnerships

Navigating the labyrinth of nonmonogamous relationships can feel like diving into uncharted waters. The map? Well, it's constantly being redrawn as you sail along. One crucial tool in your navigation kit is the art of negotiating boundaries. Think of it like drawing lines in the sand, but, you know, with a lot more conversation and a lot less drama.

***Setting the Scene**

Picture this: you and your partner have decided to explore the vast seas of nonmonogamy. Excitement bubbles up, but so does a touch of anxiety. How do you even begin to discuss the boundaries that will keep your ship afloat? Start by taking a deep breath. This is a journey you're embarking on together, and communication is your North Star.

***The Compass of Communication**

When it comes to negotiating boundaries, your communication compass needs to be finely tuned. Start with an open dialogue about your desires, fears, and expectations. Imagine you're sharing a meal together – comfort is key. No need for formalities or highbrow language; just talk like you would about your favorite movie or that weird dream you had last night.

"Hey, babe, so I was thinking about this whole nonmonogamy thing. What are your thoughts on it? No pressure, just curious."

See? Simple. Lay your cards on the table, and encourage your partner to do the same. It's not a game of poker; it's a cooperative game where both players win.

***The Art of Boundaries**
 Now, let's dive into the nitty-gritty of boundaries. It's not about building walls; it's about crafting bridges that connect your desires with your partner's. Imagine you're both architects designing a love nest that fits both your tastes. What kind of rooms do you need, and how much space are you comfortable sharing?

"I was thinking I'm okay with you exploring connections, but let's keep the home fires burning. No overnights, at least for now. What are your thoughts?"

Feel free to sketch, erase, and redraw until you've created a blueprint that feels just right. It's an evolving process – the blueprint might need a few edits as you sail through different relationship landscapes.

*Compassion, Not Control

Remember, boundaries aren't about control; they're about compassion. It's not a checklist to monitor your partner's every move. Instead, it's a roadmap that respects your individual needs and ensures you're both on the same page.

"Hey, I know we talked about this, but I'm feeling a bit uneasy. Can we revisit our boundaries and tweak a few things?"

Flexibility is your ally. Just as the tide changes, so might your feelings and comfort zones. Keep those lines of communication open, and be ready to adjust your sails as needed.

*Weathering the Storms

In the vast sea of nonmonogamy, storms are inevitable. Jealousy might rear its head, or insecurities might send waves crashing against your ship. This is where your negotiated boundaries become your anchor. They're not there to restrict but to reassure.

"Hey, I'm feeling a bit off about last night. Can we talk and maybe reassess our boundaries?"

See, it's not a blame game; it's a gentle recalibration of your course. It's about weathering the storms together, hand in hand, ensuring that the foundations you've laid are sturdy enough to withstand the occasional tempest.

***The Never-ending Voyage**
And so, the journey continues. Negotiating boundaries in nonmonogamous partnerships isn't a one-time deal; it's an ongoing voyage of self-discovery and shared understanding. It's about finding joy in each other's adventures and comfort in the haven you've co-created.

So, fellow explorers, may your compass always point toward open communication, your sails be filled with understanding, and your love be the guiding star in this uncharted sea of nonmonogamy. Fair winds and following seas!

Building Trust Through Effective Communication

Building trust through effective communication is like constructing a sturdy bridge between hearts—no blueprints, just honest conversations and a solid foundation of understanding. Picture this: you're on a road trip with someone, and the GPS suddenly goes on vacation. You don't panic; you pull over, unfold the map, and talk about where you want to go. Trust is that roadmap, and communication is the dialogue that ensures you're on the same page.

First things first, let's toss the idea of one-size-fits-all communication out the window. Effective communication is not a generic manual—it's a personalized dance. Get to know your partner's rhythm, quirks, and even those spontaneous twirls. It's not about what you say but how you say it, the non-verbal cues, and the spaces between the words.

Imagine you're playing a game of catch. One person throws the ball (shares a thought), and the other catches it (listens), then throws it back (responds). The key is to keep the ball in the air. Dropping it once in a while is normal; we're only human. The magic is in picking it up gracefully and continuing the game.

Now, let's talk about the elephant in the room—vulnerability. It's like opening up your treasure chest of feelings and letting someone peek inside. It's scary, but it's the real stuff. Showcasing your vulnerabilities isn't a weakness; it's a trust exercise. It says, "Hey, I trust you with the messy parts of me." And guess what? The other person might just reciprocate, turning the conversation into a beautiful, messy collaboration.

Ever noticed how a simple "I'm here for you" can feel like a warm blanket on a chilly day? That's the power of reassurance. Building trust involves being a reliable lighthouse in the storm, a consistent presence. Make promises you can keep, and when you can't, communicate why. It's like weathering the storm together, holding onto the mast, and saying, "We've got this, and I've got you."

Now, let's talk about active listening. It's not just nodding and saying, "Uh-huh." It involves paying attention, taking in what the other person is saying, and reacting in a way that goes beyond simply speaking. It distinguishes between hearing and actual listening. Recall the specifics and the small things they say, and then surprise them later on by demonstrating that you were observant. That's the kind gesture that conveys, "I appreciate what you have to say."

Conversely, if you are the one sharing, don't be hesitant to solicit criticism. Similar to altering a boat's sails, you both must be traveling in the same direction. Pose queries such as "Am I making sense?" or "How does that resonate with you?" It's a request for the other individual to accompany you on this understanding journey.

Lastly, the art of compromise. Think of it as a two-way street where both parties bring snacks for the road. You might prefer a pit stop at a cozy café, while your partner envisions a picnic under the stars. Find the middle ground; it's where the most memorable adventures happen.

In the grand scheme of things, building trust through effective communication is an ongoing project.

There's no ribbon-cutting ceremony because it's a living, breathing entity. It's about learning, growing, and evolving together, turning the pages of your shared story. So, grab that metaphorical hammer and nails, and let's build a bridge of trust that can withstand any storm, with laughter echoing across its sturdy structure.

Chapter 7: Attachment-Informed Intimacy

Attachment-informed intimacy is the secret sauce that makes relationships pop. It's like a personalized playlist of emotional connections, syncing perfectly with the rhythm of consensual nonmonogamy. Imagine it as the emotional GPS navigating the rollercoaster of love – understanding each other's attachment styles is like decoding a love language. You're not just getting cozy; you're building a fortress of feels. It's about recognizing when your partner needs a virtual hug, or when they crave a deep heart-to-heart chat. Attachment-informed intimacy is the art of weaving closeness through understanding, creating a symphony of secure bonds. It's the dance of vulnerability, where partners twirl through emotional spaces, knowing they're caught in the safety net of mutual attachment. Forget generic romance – attachment-informed intimacy is a bespoke emotional wardrobe, tailored for each unique relationship, making consensual nonmonogamy a thrilling adventure of heart connections.

Intimacy Beyond Monogamy

Intimacy beyond monogamy is like uncovering a hidden world of connection, a place where relationships stretch and breathe, refusing to be confined to the conventional molds we're so used to. It's not about straying from the path of commitment; it's about rewriting the rules, tearing down the walls, and allowing intimacy to take on a shape uniquely its own.

In the realm of nonmonogamous connections, intimacy becomes this vibrant, evolving dance. It's not a solo performance; it's a symphony, with multiple instruments playing in harmony. Each note, each moment of shared vulnerability, contributes to a melody that's richer, deeper, and somehow more authentic.

Picture this: intimacy in nonmonogamy is like a buffet of emotions. You're not stuck with the same dish day in and day out; instead, you get to savor a variety of flavors. There's the excitement of a new connection, the comfort of a familiar one, and the sweet surprise when those worlds collide. It's about having the freedom to explore different facets of yourself and your partners without judgment or restraint.

In these relationships, intimacy isn't a scarce resource to be hoarded; it's an abundant river that flows generously. It's the late-night conversations that transcend boundaries, the stolen glances across a crowded room, and the shared laughter that echoes through the intertwined stories of multiple hearts.

What makes intimacy beyond monogamy so intriguing is its adaptability. It's not a one-size-fits-all scenario; it's a bespoke suit tailored to the unique contours of each relationship. The emotional landscape is vast, and the terrain is ever-changing. Sometimes it's deep, like diving into the ocean of your partner's soul; other times, it's light, like dancing on the surface of shared laughter.

Trust becomes the currency of intimacy in nonmonogamous realms. It's the glue that holds the delicate fabric of multiple connections together. It's not just about faithfulness to one person; it's about trust in the process, trust in open communication, and trust in the resilience of the human heart.

Jealousy and insecurity? They're not the villains in this story; they're more like unexpected guests at a party. Instead of shutting them out, nonmonogamous intimacy invites them in for a chat. It's about understanding the roots of these emotions and addressing them head-on, transforming them from disruptors into catalysts for growth.

So, here's to the untamed, uncharted territory of intimacy beyond monogamy. It's a journey where the destination is ever-shifting, and the joy is in the exploration. It's about rewriting the narrative, embracing the unconventional, and discovering that the heart has an infinite capacity for connection.

Emotional Intimacy and Attachment Bonds

Emotional intimacy and attachment bonds – now that's where the magic happens in any relationship. It's like the secret sauce that turns a connection from ordinary to extraordinary, you know? So, let's dive into this fascinating world of feelings and bonds, and trust me, it's a rollercoaster you'll want to be on.

Picture this: emotional intimacy is like having a backstage pass to someone's heart. It's not just about knowing their favorite color or the name of their childhood pet; it's about understanding their fears, dreams, and the quirky dance moves they only bust out when nobody's watching. It's the kind of closeness that goes beyond the surface, and it's built on a foundation of trust, vulnerability, and shared experiences.

Now, let's throw attachment bonds into the mix. Think of them as the superglue of relationships – they're what keeps you sticking together through thick and thin. Attachment bonds are like emotional safety nets; they make you feel secure, wanted, and valued. It's that reassuring feeling that says, "Hey, no matter what happens, we've got each other's backs."

So, how do these two dance partners – emotional intimacy and attachment bonds – tango together? Well, it starts with openness. You've got to be willing to peel back the layers, share your deepest thoughts, and be there for your partner when they do the same. It's a beautiful exchange, like passing notes in class but on a much deeper, soulful level.

Trust is the VIP guest at this party. Without trust, emotional intimacy and attachment bonds just stumble around awkwardly. Trust is earned through small gestures, keeping promises, and showing up when it matters. It's the bridge that connects your emotional islands, making sure you're never too far apart.

Now, Vulnerability is the emotional intimacy equivalent of a superhero costume. Being open and vulnerable is a strength rather than a weakness. Saying, "This is who I am—flaws and all." You may bring your partner into the authentic, messy, and beautiful aspects of your life when you give yourself permission to be vulnerable. Saying "I trust you enough to show you the unfiltered me" is analogous to this.

Shared experiences are the spice of life, and they're the secret ingredient to attachment bonds. Whether it's traveling to a new place, conquering a cooking disaster together, or just binge-watching your favorite show on a lazy Sunday, those shared moments create a unique language that only the two of you understand. It's the silent jokes, the knowing glances – your own little universe.

And here's the kicker – emotional intimacy and attachment bonds aren't one-size-fits-all. Every relationship has its own rhythm, its own dance. It's about finding what works for you and your partner. Maybe it's late-night talks, handwritten notes, or simply holding hands while walking. Whatever it is, make it yours.

In the end, this dance between emotional intimacy and attachment bonds is a lifelong journey. It's not about reaching a destination; it's about enjoying the dance itself. So, put on your favorite song, take your partner's hand, and let the music of emotional intimacy and attachment bonds serenade your unique love story.

Maintaining Connection in Nonmonogamous Configurations

Alright, let's dive into the world of maintaining a connection in nonmonogamous configurations. Picture this: relationships are like delicate plants. They need the right nutrients, sunlight, and, most importantly, a bit of tending to thrive. Now, throw in the nonmonogamous twist, and it's like managing a garden with multiple exotic flowers. Intriguing, right?

***The Dance of Communication**
First things first, communication is the heartbeat of any relationship, and in the world of nonmonogamy, it's like the rhythm section of a great band. You've got to be in sync. Discuss your needs, wants, and feelings in an honest and open manner. This is not a soliloquy; it's a two-way street. Share your thoughts, and more importantly, listen. That's the secret sauce to maintaining a connection that withstands the twists and turns of nonmonogamous living.

***The Art of Checking In**
Imagine you're sailing the relationship seas, exploring uncharted territories. Regular check-ins are your compass. Take a moment to sit down, look at the map together, and discuss how you're navigating these waters. Are there storms on the

horizon? Smooth sailing ahead? Checking in isn't about finding problems; it's about making sure everyone's on board with the journey.

***Navigating Jealousy Waters**
Ah, jealousy – the tumultuous sea that can capsize the sturdiest ships. In the world of nonmonogamy, it's essential to acknowledge jealousy, not as an enemy but as a curious passenger on this journey. Share your feelings, and don't be afraid to ask for reassurance. It's like handing out life jackets – you're in this together, ensuring everyone stays afloat.

***Building Bridges, Not Walls**
Imagine your relationships as interconnected bridges. Each connection strengthens the overall structure. In non-monogamous configurations, it's not about building walls to separate partners; it's about constructing sturdy, supportive bridges. Encourage your partners to form meaningful connections. Share the joy, and celebrate the connections – it's the architectural marvel of polyamorous love.

***Embracing Individual Growth**

Nonmonogamous setups are like personalized gyms for personal growth. Encourage each other's individual journeys. Your partner taking salsa classes with someone else doesn't diminish your dance – it enriches it. Embrace the beauty of personal evolution within the larger landscape of your relationship. It's not a competition; it's a symphony of growth.

***Laughter – The Universal Solvent**
In the grand scheme of things, laughter is the WD-40 of relationships. It loosens up the tight spots and keeps the gears moving smoothly. In nonmonogamy, find joy in the quirks, relish the shared moments, and laugh together. It's the elixir that turns potential awkwardness into shared jokes and shared jokes into lasting memories.

***Time: The Currency of Connection**
In the realm of nonmonogamy, time is your most precious currency. Invest it wisely. Schedule date nights, whether they're with one partner or all partners involved. Quality time is like watering your relationship garden – it helps everything bloom. And remember, it's not about equal time for everyone; it's

about equitable time based on needs and agreements.

As I go... Oh, Wait, There Isn't One

And there you have it – a glimpse into the art of maintaining a connection in nonmonogamous configurations. It's a dance, a journey, and an ongoing conversation. Embrace the uniqueness, revel in the shared experiences, and remember, there's no one-size-fits-all guide. So, go forth, tend to your relationship garden, and let the love flourish in all its diverse and beautiful forms.

Chapter 8 Challenges and Solutions.

In this chapter, we dive into the rollercoaster of challenges that come with juggling multiple relationships in a world that often favors the simplicity of monogamy. Picture this: jealousy creeping in like an unexpected guest at a party, communication breakdowns resembling a game of broken telephone, and the ever-present fear of attachment insecurities playing the background soundtrack. But fear not! We're not here to just outline problems; we're your trusty navigators through the storm. Learn how to turn jealousy into a catalyst for growth, unravel the mysteries of effective communication that even your grandma would be proud of, and discover ingenious ways to nurture secure bonds amid the chaos. It's like having a backstage pass to the concert of nonmonogamous relationships, where we not only expose the hurdles but hand you the VIP solutions to make your journey truly epic. Get ready for an unforgettable experience.

Jealousy and Insecurity in Polysecure Relationships

Jealousy and insecurity – two uninvited guests that often show up at the nonmonogamous relationship party. Let's be real, navigating these emotional minefields can feel like trying to defuse a bomb while blindfolded. But fear not, fellow poly explorers, because we're about to embark on a journey through the tangled vines of jealousy and the swampy marshes of insecurity in the realm of polysecure relationships.

First off, let's acknowledge the elephant in the room – jealousy is a thing, and it doesn't discriminate. It doesn't care if you've got a dozen partners or if you've read all the books on ethical nonmonogamy. Jealousy can rear its green-eyed head when you least expect it, and suddenly you're knee-deep in a pit of emotions, wondering how the heck you got there.

Picture this: Your partner comes home, their eyes sparkling from an evening with someone else. The initial reaction? A pang of jealousy that hits you like an unexpected wave. You start questioning everything – your own worth, your connection with your partner, and whether you should just throw in the towel and become a hermit.

But let's pump the brakes on the doom and gloom for a sec. Jealousy isn't the enemy; it's more like that annoying friend who doesn't know when to leave the party. It's a signal, a flashing neon sign pointing to something deeper. Maybe it's a need for reassurance, a desire for more quality time, or just a reminder that, hey, you're pretty awesome too.

Now, insecurity, oh sweet insecurity – the sneaky saboteur of self-esteem. It whispers doubts in your ear, plays tricks on your mind, and before you know it, you're comparing yourself to every other person in your poly circle. "Am I attractive enough? Am I interested? Do they like them more than me?" Cue the mental circus.

But here's the real deal: Insecurity is a shape-shifter. It changes form based on the insecurities we carry with us. The antidote? Radical self-love. Embrace your quirks, celebrate your uniqueness, and remember that you bring something special to the table – something no one else does.

So, how do we dance with these unruly partners without stepping on toes? Communication, my friends, is the key to the nonmonogamous tango. Talk about your feelings, lay your vulnerabilities on the table, and let your partner know when the green-eyed monster comes knocking. Vulnerability is not weakness; it's the glue that holds the intricate web of poly-secure connections together.

And hey, jealousy can even be a catalyst for growth. Use it as an opportunity to explore your own desires, communicate your needs, and strengthen the bond you share with your partners. In the grand symphony of polyamory, jealousy is just one instrument – and when played in harmony, it can create a beautiful melody of understanding and connection.

Insecurity? Well, treat it like that annoying song that gets stuck in your head. Replace it with a self-love anthem and dance to the rhythm of your own worth. Remember, you're not just navigating nonmonogamy; you're crafting a unique, polysecure masterpiece that's as dynamic and ever-changing as the relationships within it.

Navigating Jealousy and Insecurity

Ever found yourself tangled in the vines of jealousy, wondering how the heck you ended up in this emotional thicket? Welcome to the jungle, my friend. In this chapter, we're going to hack our way through the dense foliage of insecurity and navigate the wild terrain of nonmonogamous emotions. So grab your metaphorical machete, and let's get started.

***Understanding the Green-Eyed Monster**
Jealousy – the sneaky critter that can slink into even the most secure hearts. It's okay; we've all been there. Instead of pretending it doesn't exist, let's acknowledge that jealousy is as human as double-dipping your fries. We'll dissect what triggers it and how to recognize its footprints before it pounces.

***The Insecurity Swamp: A Treacherous Landscape**
Ever feel like you're wading through a swamp of self-doubt? You're not alone. Insecurity is that murky water that can make you question your worth and leave you knee-deep in doubt. Together, we'll

find solid ground, build bridges over the swamp, and pave a path toward a more confident you.

*Mapping Your Emotions: X Marks the Spot

What's the treasure hidden in the emotional map of jealousy and insecurity? Spoiler alert: it's self-awareness. We'll chart your emotional landscape, marking where jealousy tends to rear its head and where the quicksand of insecurity lies. Once you know the terrain, you can navigate it like a seasoned explorer.

*Communication: The Compass in Your Toolkit

Communication is the compass that'll guide you out of the emotional wilderness. Learn the language to express your feelings without turning them into a wild, untamed beast. We'll explore open, honest, and compassionate ways to share your emotions, ensuring you don't get lost in translation.

*Jealousy Busters and Insecurity Repellents

Ready to fend off jealousy like a superhero swats away villains? We'll concoct your custom jealousy-busting spray and craft an insecurity repellent so effective, it'll make mosquitoes jealous. These practical tools will become your trusty sidekicks in the fight against the emotional bugs trying to bite.

***Real-Life Expeditions: Stories from the Trenches**
No adventure is complete without tales from the front lines. We'll delve into real-life stories of jealousy triumphs and insecurity vanquished. Hear from those who've navigated the emotional jungle and come out the other side with battle scars and badges of resilience.

***Stay Curious, Stay Adventurous**
Remember, the jungle of jealousy and insecurity is vast, but so is your capacity for growth. Embrace the adventure, stay curious, and let's face these emotional beasts head-on. The journey is challenging, but the view from the top of the mountain is worth every step. Onward!

Addressing Attachment-Related Conflicts

Ever had that feeling when a situation just rubs you the wrong way in your nonmonogamous relationship? It's like there's this emotional knot that tightens, and you're left wondering, "What just happened?" Well, my poly pals, you've likely stumbled upon an attachment-related conflict. Don't worry; it's not the end of the world. In fact, it might just be the beginning of a growth spurt in your relationship. So, grab a comfy seat, and let's dive into untangling these emotional spaghetti noodles together.

***Attachment Knots: Unraveling the Tangle**
Attachments can be tricky. We all have different needs, expectations, and quirks. Sometimes, our attachment styles collide like two poorly programmed robots on a collision course. Picture this: You're feeling a bit distant, your partner is craving closeness, and bam! You've got an attachment-related conflict ready to serve. It's like a sitcom plot, but with more emotional baggage.

Step 1: Recognize the Knots
The first step in dealing with attachment-related conflicts is acknowledging their existence. It's easy to sweep these feelings under the rug, but that rug will eventually bulge like a lumpy mattress, making

everyone uncomfortable. So, pause, take a breath, and say, "Houston, we've got a problem."

Step 2: The Art of Listening (Without Eye Rolls)
Communication is the superhero here, but not the kind that wears a cape. It's the subtle, everyday hero that saves relationships. When your partner is expressing their attachment needs, resist the eye roll. Instead, listen actively. Ask questions. Repeat back what you heard. It's not rocket science; it's empathy in action.

Step 3: The Vulnerability Dance
Here's the secret sauce – vulnerability. It's like a dance; someone takes the lead, shares a bit of themselves, and then it's your turn. In attachment conflicts, it's about exposing those tender spots, saying, "Hey, I'm feeling a bit scared here." Vulnerability creates connection. It's the antidote to attachment conflicts.

Step 4: Negotiate, Don't Dictate
Now, let's talk solutions. Remember, it's not about one person's way or the highway. It's about finding common ground. Negotiate like you're brokering a

peace deal – compromise, find a middle ground, and remember that you're a team. Dictating terms might win a battle, but it loses the relationship war.

Step 5: Rinse and Repeat
Addressing attachment-related conflicts isn't a one-and-done deal. It's more like laundry – a perpetual cycle. So, get comfortable with the fact that conflicts will happen. It's a sign of growth but not failure. Rinse, repeat, and keep those emotional garments fresh.

***In the Attachment Arena: A Personal Anecdote**
Let me share a little secret. My partner and I once found ourselves in the middle of an attachment tug-of-war. Instead of seeing it as a disaster, we turned it into a learning experience. We laughed about our quirks, hugged out the tension, and coined a silly term for our attachment dance. Now, when things get sticky, we just say, "Looks like we're doing the Attachment Cha-Cha again."

So, there you have it, poly pals. Attachment conflicts are like the unexpected guests at your nonmonogamous party. Embrace them, dance with them, and turn the conflict chaos into a beautifully messy masterpiece of connection. Happy dancing!

Nurturing Secure Bonds in a Nonmonogamous Lifestyle

Alright, let's talk about something real: building rock-solid connections in the world of non-monogamy. Because, let's face it, navigating multiple relationships ain't a walk in the park, but it can be one heck of a fulfilling journey. So, how do we go about nurturing secure bonds when the love web extends beyond just two?

1. Communication: It's the Non-Secret Sauce

First things first, we're diving headfirst into the deep ocean of communication. No, we're not talking about the generic "we need to talk." We're talking about the good stuff – the kind where honesty and openness are the superheroes. In nonmonogamy, these two are your power couple. Lay it all out on the table – expectations, fears, dreams. No room for assumptions, pal.

2. Boundaries: The Unseen Guardians

Picture this: boundaries are like invisible bodyguards for your relationship. Establish them. Respect them. If you're not sure, ask. It's like navigating a complex dance – each partner has their unique moves, and it's crucial to sync up. Consent is your compass here. Check-in regularly and adjust the dance steps if needed.

3. Jealousy: The Uninvited Guest

Ah, the green-eyed monster – jealousy. It happens, and that's okay. Acknowledge it, don't shove it under the rug. Instead of pointing fingers, explore the why. Is it a need for more time, attention, or something else? Share those feelings. It's not about blame but understanding and finding solutions together.

4. Quality Over Quantity

In nonmonogamy, it's not about collecting relationships like Pokémon cards. Quality always trumps quantity. Invest time and emotional energy wisely. Connect deeply, understand your partners on a profound level, and let them know they matter. It's about the richness of connection, not the sheer number of connections.

5. Emotional Check-Ins: Like Vitamins for Relationships

Just like you take vitamins to stay healthy, relationships need regular emotional check-ins. How are you feeling? How are they feeling? It's the small things – a random "How was your day?" text or a heartfelt "I appreciate you." These moments build a foundation of emotional security, making your relationship fortress resilient.

6. Supporting Independence: You Do You

In nonmonogamy, it's not about possessing someone but celebrating their individuality. Support your partners in their personal pursuits and encourage their growth. The more secure and fulfilled individuals are within themselves, the stronger the collective bond becomes.

7. Learn from Mistakes: They're the Best Teachers

Let's face it, we all stumble. In nonmonogamy, it's not about avoiding mistakes but learning from them. Apologize when necessary, forgive when possible, and grow together. It's the messy parts that often lead to the most significant breakthroughs.

8. Riding the Waves of Change:

In any relationship, change is the only constant. Nonmonogamous bonds are no exception. Be open to evolving together, and view change as an opportunity for growth. Sometimes it's a gentle breeze, and other times it's a storm, but facing it hand in hand builds resilience. Whether exploring new dynamics or adapting to shifting emotions, viewing change as a shared journey keeps the connection alive and vibrant.

9. Celebrating Each Unique Connection:

In the tapestry of nonmonogamous relationships, each thread is unique, creating a pattern that's entirely your own. Celebrate the individual connections you share with each partner. It's not a competition; it's a mosaic of love, respect, and understanding. Embrace the beauty in the diversity of your bonds, recognizing that each one contributes to the richness of your relationship landscape.

10. Cherishing the Present Moment:

In the whirlwind of nonmonogamous living, it's easy to get caught up in what's next or what's happened before. Ground yourselves in the present moment. Whether you're sharing a quiet morning coffee or navigating a complex emotional terrain, being fully present enhances the connection. It's the magic ingredient that elevates commonplace experiences into unforgettable ones.

So, there you have it – a roadmap to weaving a tapestry of secure bonds in the nonmonogamous realm. It's an ongoing journey, an adventure with twists and turns, but oh, the stories you'll collect along the way. Cheers to building something extraordinary!

Chapter 9 Cultural and Societal Perspectives

In the rollercoaster of poly-secure relationships, buckle up for the Cultural and Societal Perspectives ride! Imagine navigating nonmonogamy across diverse cultural landscapes – it's like salsa dancing through different beats. We'll dissect how cultural norms spice up or simmer down polysecure dynamics, uncovering the unspoken rules that often lurk in the shadows. Ever wonder how your grandma's old stories might influence your modern poly love story? We'll go into the generational impact on nonmonogamous choices, unraveling traditions that might high-five or high-five-no-way your poly lifestyle. Join the journey as we unravel societal whispers and norms, unveiling how they shape, support, or challenge the very essence of consensual nonmonogamy. This chapter is your backstage pass to understanding the cultural symphony playing in the background of your polysecure relationships. Fasten your seatbelt – it's going to be a bumpy, insightful, and eye-opening ride!

Polysecure Relationships in Different Cultural Contexts

Polysecure relationships in different cultural contexts add vibrant hues to the tapestry of human connection. Imagine a world where love and attachment dance to the beat of diverse traditions and societal norms. Let's embark on a journey to unravel the unique intricacies of polyamory across cultures, where relationships are not just about the connection between two, but a harmonious blend of individuals within a larger societal canvas.

In the heart of Paris, the City of Love takes on a new meaning as polysecure relationships gracefully navigate the cobblestone streets. French culture, known for its openness to matters of the heart, sees polyamory as a nuanced expression of freedom. Café conversations buzz with laughter, as Parisians effortlessly weave attachments, entangling hearts in a sophisticated dance of emotions. Here, polyamory is not a rebellion; it's a canvas where love paints its own masterpiece.

On the contrary, in the bustling streets of Tokyo, the rhythm of polysecure relationships mirrors the precision of a well-choreographed dance. Japanese culture, deeply rooted in tradition, embraces polyamory with quiet respect. The concept of "compersion" is delicately woven into the cultural fabric, emphasizing the joy derived from a partner's happiness with others. Relationships in Tokyo are an art form, with partners co-creating a masterpiece of emotional interconnectedness.

Venture into the heart of Rio de Janeiro, and you'll find polysecure relationships moving to the lively beats of samba. Brazilian culture, renowned for its celebration of passion, welcomes polyamory as an expression of the soul's desire for connection. The warmth of Brazilian embraces extends beyond monogamous boundaries, creating a carnival of love where attachment knows no limits. In this cultural landscape, polyamory is not a departure from tradition; it's a colorful evolution.

In the vibrant streets of Mumbai, polysecure relationships take on a Bollywood twist, where emotions run high, and love conquers all. Indian culture, a tapestry of diverse traditions, sees polyamory as an exploration of the heart's capacity to love abundantly. Amidst the aromas of spices and the vibrant colors of sarees, relationships become a dance of interconnected souls, guided by the ancient rhythms of Kama Sutra.

Zooming into the quiet lanes of Stockholm, polysecure relationships in the Nordic embrace embody the concept of "hygge." Swedish culture, with its emphasis on comfort and coziness, fosters relationships built on mutual understanding and consent. Polyamory here is a pragmatic extension of this ethos, where individuals craft relationships as warm and inviting as a crackling fireplace on a winter evening.

As we traverse the globe, it becomes evident that polysecure relationships are not a one-size-fits-all affair. Each culture adds its own brushstroke to the canvas of love, creating a rich and diverse panorama of human connection. Whether in the romantic alleys of Paris or the bustling streets of Tokyo, polyamory adapts, evolves, and flourishes, proving that love is indeed a universal language spoken in myriad dialects.

Societal Norms and Their Impact on Nonmonogamous Attachments

Picture this: you're at a backyard barbecue, sipping on your drink of choice, surrounded by laughter and the smell of grilling burgers. Now, imagine dropping into the conversation that you're in a nonmonogamous relationship. What kind of attitude do you think you'd get? Cheers, applause, or maybe just a few awkward coughs? Societal norms have a way of casting a spotlight on our relationships, and when it comes to nonmonogamy, that spotlight can feel more like a laser beam.

The Perceived Threat to Tradition
Let's face it – society loves its traditions. From white picket fences to happily-ever-afters, we've been handed a script on what our love lives should look like. Deviating from this script? Well, that's like coloring outside the lines of a cherished family portrait. Nonmonogamy, in its various forms,

challenges the status quo, and society doesn't always respond with open arms.

Whispers and Raised Eyebrows

Drop the term "polyamory" in a casual conversation, and you might catch a few raised eyebrows or hesitant glances. Why? Because we're accustomed to narratives that revolve around one person, one love. The societal whispers start: "Isn't that just another word for cheating?" or "Can't people just commit anymore?" Nonmonogamous attachments often face scrutiny simply because they defy the norm.

The Fear of the Unknown

Societal norms act as a safety net. We know what to expect, and anything straying too far from the norm can trigger discomfort. Nonmonogamy introduces a level of unpredictability that can be unsettling for those who thrive on the security of tradition. It's like trying to explain a color that no one has ever seen — it's met with skepticism until proven otherwise.

Labeling and Stereotyping

In a society that loves labels, nonmonogamous relationships often find themselves stuck with ones that don't quite fit. "Commitment-phobic," "reckless," or "immoral" are just a few labels thrown around. But behind these labels are real people navigating the complex terrain of love and attachment. It's not about avoiding commitment; it's about redefining what commitment means.

The Unseen Pressures

Dig a little deeper, and you'll find the unseen pressures that societal norms place on nonmonogamous attachments. There's a constant need to justify, explain, and prove that unconventional love can be just as deep, meaningful, and committed as its monogamous counterpart. It's a battle against preconceived notions, fought one conversation at a time.

A Call for Acceptance

As we navigate the minefield of societal norms, it's worth questioning why we hold onto certain expectations. Nonmonogamous attachments may challenge tradition, but they also open the door to a richer tapestry of love. The real revolution lies not just in reshaping relationships but in fostering a society where love is celebrated in all its forms, even the rebellious ones.

So, the next time someone mentions their nontraditional love story, maybe swap the raised eyebrow for a curious smile. After all, love rebels are just trying to find their own happily ever after in a world that's still learning to embrace the beautifully unconventional.

Shifting Paradigms: The Future of Polysecure Relationships

Alright, let's dive into the exciting world of where polysecure relationships are headed. Buckle up, because we're not just talking about your grandma's relationship advice here. We're breaking free from old molds, forging new paths, and embracing a future where love is as diverse as your favorite playlist.

Picture this: the future of polysecure relationships isn't just about having multiple partners. It's about creating a space where emotional safety and security take center stage. In the years to come, it's less about counting how many partners you have and more about the quality of connections you're nurturing.

Imagine a world where jealousy is an old, dusty relic of the past. We're talking about a future where open and honest communication isn't just a buzzword but a way of life. It's a place where you can say, "Hey, I'm feeling a bit off about this," and your partners respond with empathy and understanding, not judgment.

In the shifting landscape of polysecure relationships, attachment theory becomes our guiding compass. We're not just throwing around terms like "secure attachment" for the sake of it; we're living it. Partnerships are evolving into these beautiful gardens of emotional intimacy, carefully tended to with the fertilizer of trust and the sunlight of vulnerability.

But let's get real for a moment. Shifting paradigms means facing challenges. It means acknowledging that we're rewriting the relationship rulebook, and it's not always a walk in the park. The future of polysecure relationships involves navigating through uncharted territory, figuring out what works for you, and, more importantly, what doesn't.

Think about it like this: we're crafting relationships that are as unique as a fingerprint. No more cookie-cutter approaches. It's about finding what makes your heart race, what makes you feel secure, and then, boldly embracing it.

And guess what? The future of polysecure relationships isn't limited to a specific age group, gender, or culture. It's an inclusive party where everyone is invited. Love is love, and it doesn't conform to societal expectations. So, in the future, we're letting go of outdated norms and embracing the beautiful mosaic of diverse connections.

In this brave new world, societal judgments about the number of partners you have are replaced with a collective nod of understanding. The future of polysecure relationships isn't about rebellion; it's about redefining what it means to love and be loved.

So, here's to the future – a future where polysecure relationships aren't just a choice; they're a celebration of authenticity, vulnerability, and a whole lot of love. Welcome to a world where your heart can roam freely, where the only rule is to be true to yourself and the connections you hold dear.

Cheers to rewriting the script and embracing the wild, wonderful, and polysecure future ahead!

Chapter 10: The HEARTS of Being Polysecure.

Ever wondered what makes polyamorous relationships thrive? It's all in the HEARTS – not the mushy stuff, but the essential elements of being Polysecure. "H" stands for Healthy Attachments. We delve into Attachment Theory, dissecting how it shapes the very foundation of secure connections in a poly landscape. Moving on to "E" for Embracing Polyfidelity, we explore the intricacies of exclusive commitment within consensual nonmonogamy. "A" is for Addressing Trauma, because let's face it, we've all got a bit of baggage. Unpacking and healing are crucial for maintaining a solid poly foundation.

Now, let's talk about "R" – Communication and Relationship Resilience. In poly life, open lines and resilience are as essential as morning coffee. "T" is for Trust, the glue holding it all together. We'll discuss how trust is earned, shattered, and rebuilt in the poly arena. Lastly, "S" represents Secure Bonds, not just between partners but within the entire poly web. It's a journey through the HEARTS, unlocking the secrets of Polysecurity for a love life that beats strong and true.

Alright, buckle up, because we're about to dive into the juicy center of being polysecure. We're not talking about just the logistics or the rules; we're getting right to the heart of the matter – the emotional epicenter, if you will.

Picture this: a bustling emotional hub where trust, communication, and vulnerability intersect. That's where the magic happens in polysecure relationships. Let's unpack the HEARTS of being polysecure:

1. Honesty: First things first, let's talk about keeping it real. In the world of polysecurity, honesty isn't just about saying what you had for lunch. It's about baring your soul, being transparent about your feelings, desires, and, yeah, maybe your weird habits too. It's creating a space where truth is the currency, and everyone's a billionaire.

2. Empathy: Now, empathy isn't just a fancy word we throw around in self-help books. It's the secret sauce of polysecurity. It's about understanding that your partner's feelings are as valid as yours, even if they have a completely different emotional playlist. It's the ability to step into their shoes without losing your own. Think of it as emotional multitasking.

3. Affection: Ah, the sweet stuff. We're not just talking about physical affection (although that's important too), but the kind that says, "I've got your back." It's the whispered "I love you" in the middle of the night, the reassuring touch when things get rocky, and the shared laughter that makes your heart do a happy dance.

4. Resilience: Relationships are like roller coasters – full of twists, turns, and the occasional loop-de-loop. Being polysecure isn't about avoiding the bumps; it's about bouncing back when life throws you a curveball. It's the resilience to weather storms together, knowing that every rough patch is a chance to grow stronger.

5. Trust: Consider trust the cornerstone of the polysecure temple. It's not just about trusting that your partner won't swipe the last slice of pizza (though that's crucial too), but trusting them with your fears, your dreams, and your vulnerabilities. It's the unwavering belief that you're in this together, no matter what.

6. Security: Last but certainly not least, let's talk about security. We're not talking about passwords or fingerprint scans. It's the emotional security that comes from knowing you're valued, respected, and cherished. It's creating a haven where you can let down your guard without fearing judgment.

In the heart of polysecurity, it's not about building walls; it's about constructing a love fortress that can withstand the test of time and the occasional emotional earthquake. These HEARTS are the compass that guides you through the labyrinth of consensual nonmonogamy. So, put on your emotional armor, grab your partner's hand, and let's navigate this polysecure adventure together.

Chapter 11: The S in the HEARTS-Secure Attachment With Self

Ah, the 'S' in HEARTS – Secure Attachment with Self! Now, buckle up because we're diving into the good stuff – the kind of self-love that's not just about spa days and bubble baths (although, those are pretty great too).

Picture this: You're the main character in the movie of your life, and the 'S' is like the plot twist where you learn to be your own superhero. Secure Attachment to Self is like having a personal cheerleader inside your head, a constant supporter who's got your back, rain or shine.

Let's break it down. Secure Attachment with Self is all about being BFFs with you – flaws, quirks, and all. It's about understanding that your worth isn't tied to external validation or Instagram likes. Nope, your worth is like this rock-solid foundation, unshaken by the storms of self-doubt.

Think of it as treating yourself like you would your best friend. If your friend messes up, you wouldn't throw them under the bus, right? So, why do it to yourself? Secure Attachment with Self is that gentle voice saying, "Hey, we all make mistakes. Let's learn and grow from this."

But, oh, it's not just about the mistakes. It's also about celebrating the victories, big or small. Got out of bed today? High five! Finished a project at work? Fist bump! Secure Attachment with Self is that friend who throws confetti for your achievements, reminding you that you're a rockstar.

Now, let's talk about the inner chatter – you know, that ongoing conversation in your mind. Secure Attachment to Self is like upgrading that chatter from a cranky radio station to a feel-good playlist. It's about turning down the volume on self-criticism and turning up the love and encouragement.

And here's the secret sauce – self-compassion. It's not about being perfect; it's about being perfectly human. Secure Attachment with Self is extending the same kindness to yourself that you'd offer a friend going through a tough time. You wouldn't kick them when they're down, right? So, be your own gentle hand to lift yourself up.

In a world that often tells us to be everything for everyone else, Secure Attachment with Self is that rebel yell, saying, "Hey, take care of yourself too!" It's setting boundaries, recognizing your needs, and unapologetically putting yourself first when necessary.

So, here's the bottom line: Secure Attachment to Self is the anchor in the storm, the compass on your journey. It's about being your own MVP, your own biggest fan, and your own happily-ever-after. Because, my friend, you deserve that kind of love – the unshakeable, unwavering, and utterly fabulous love from the one person who will be with you every step of the way – yourself

The Continued Journey of Polysecure Attachment

So, here we are – right in the thick of it, exploring the ongoing adventure of Polysecure Attachment. Grab a seat and let's dive into the heart of what keeps these nonmonogamous connections ticking and evolving.

The Ever-Unfolding Story

You know, relationships are like stories; they don't have neat endings, just new chapters. And in the world of Polysecure Attachment, the journey is anything but predictable. It's this constant unfolding that makes it so darn fascinating.

Living in the Gray

One thing we've learned? Life's messy, and so are relationships. There's no one-size-fits-all in the world of Polysecure Attachment. It's a spectrum, a canvas waiting for you to splash your own unique colors. Forget the rigid rules; let's embrace the beautiful messiness of it all.

Embracing the Challenges

Sure, there are challenges – moments when you question if you've bitten off more than you can chew. Jealousy might rear its head, or old wounds may resurface. But guess what? That's all part of the journey. It's not about avoiding the bumps; it's about learning to navigate them. Because, my friend, growth happens in those awkward, uncomfortable spaces.

Thriving in Change

The beauty of Polysecure Attachment lies in its adaptability. As soon as you believe you have everything figured out, something unexpected happens to you. And you know what? That's the good stuff. It keeps things fresh, prevents stagnation, and opens up new avenues for connection. Embrace change, and watch your polysecure garden bloom.

Connection Beyond Boundaries

We've scratched the surface of cultural and societal influences on nonmonogamous bonds. The journey doesn't stop at personal growth; it extends to the broader landscape of acceptance and understanding. As the world evolves, so does the narrative of polysecure relationships, challenging norms and creating space for diverse love stories.

No End in Sight

So, my fellow adventurer, there's no grand finale here. We're not tying a neat bow around Polysecure Attachment because, truthfully, it's an ongoing saga. Relationships ebb and flow, and so does our understanding of them. Let's keep wandering, discovering, and embracing the beautiful mess of polysecure love. Because in the end, it's not about reaching a destination; it's about relishing every step of the journey. Cheers to the unpredictable, ever-evolving ride!

APPENDIX

Summing Up Key Findings

Summing up the key findings of our journey through the twists and turns of Polysecure relationships. Picture this as our grand finale, the moment when the curtain falls, and we get to soak in the wisdom we've gathered along the way.

*Attachment Magic

So, we started with Attachment 101. Turns out, understanding attachment styles is like having a secret decoder ring for relationships. We've got the anxious, the avoidant, the secure—each with its unique flavor. It's like the salsa of the emotional world, and how we dance through it determines a lot about our connections.

*Trauma, the Sneaky Guest

Trauma, our uninvited party crasher. We can't ignore it; it's there, affecting our dance moves. But here's the twist: acknowledging it, facing it, allows us to reclaim the dance floor. Trauma-informed relationships? They're like putting on the perfect pair of dancing shoes—comfortable, supportive, and damn stylish.

*Polyamory: More Love, More Responsibility

Then we waltzed into the world of consensual nonmonogamy. It's not just about throwing more people into the relationship mix; it's a strategic, mindful tango. Communication, trust, and a sprinkle of vulnerability are our secret weapons. Imagine it as a potluck dinner where everyone brings their best dish—spicy, sweet, and sometimes a little unexpected.

*Talking the Talk in Poly Land

Communication took the spotlight, and boy, did it shine. Open and honest conversations are the heartbeat of these relationships. It's not just about talking; it's about speaking a language of emotions and understanding the nuances of each other's narratives. Negotiating boundaries? That's like setting the house rules for our emotional party.

*Intimacy: More Than Skin Deep

Our exploration of intimacy wasn't just about the physical. Emotional intimacy is the real soul food. It's about baring our hearts and connecting on a level that goes beyond the surface. Think of it as the difference between a quick high-five and a warm, lingering hug.

*Navigating Storms in the Sea of Jealousy

Jealousy? Ah, the storm that can rock even the sturdiest relationship boat. But guess what? We learned to ride those waves. Understanding the roots, facing it head-on, and turning jealousy into a compass guiding us towards growth.

*Polysecure in Different Shades and Colors

Cultural and societal perspectives gave us a kaleidoscope of Polysecure relationships. It's not a one-size-fits-all deal; it's a vibrant tapestry, woven with threads of diverse norms and values. From one culture to another, from society's raised eyebrows to accepting nods, we witnessed the spectrum.

And there you have it, the grand mosaic of Polysecure relationships. It's not just a lifestyle; it's an evolving, dynamic masterpiece. As we bid adieu to this rollercoaster ride, let's carry these lessons in our backpack of experiences, ready for the next adventure in the ever-expanding universe of human connections. Cheers to the polysecure dance—we've learned the steps, and stumbled a bit, but oh, what a dance it has been!

NOTES

NOTES

NOTES

NOTES

NOTES

NOTES

NOTES

NOTES

NOTES

NOTES

www.ingramcontent.com/pod-product-compliance
Lightning Source LLC
Chambersburg PA
CBHW070947260726
48661CB00003B/1167